Adult Coloring Book
Dogs

Detailed, Intricate, Stress Relief Dog Pattern Coloring Designs for Adults and Grown-Ups

Mia Blackwood

www.southshorepublications.com

ISBN-13: 978-1519558244
ISBN-10: 1519558244

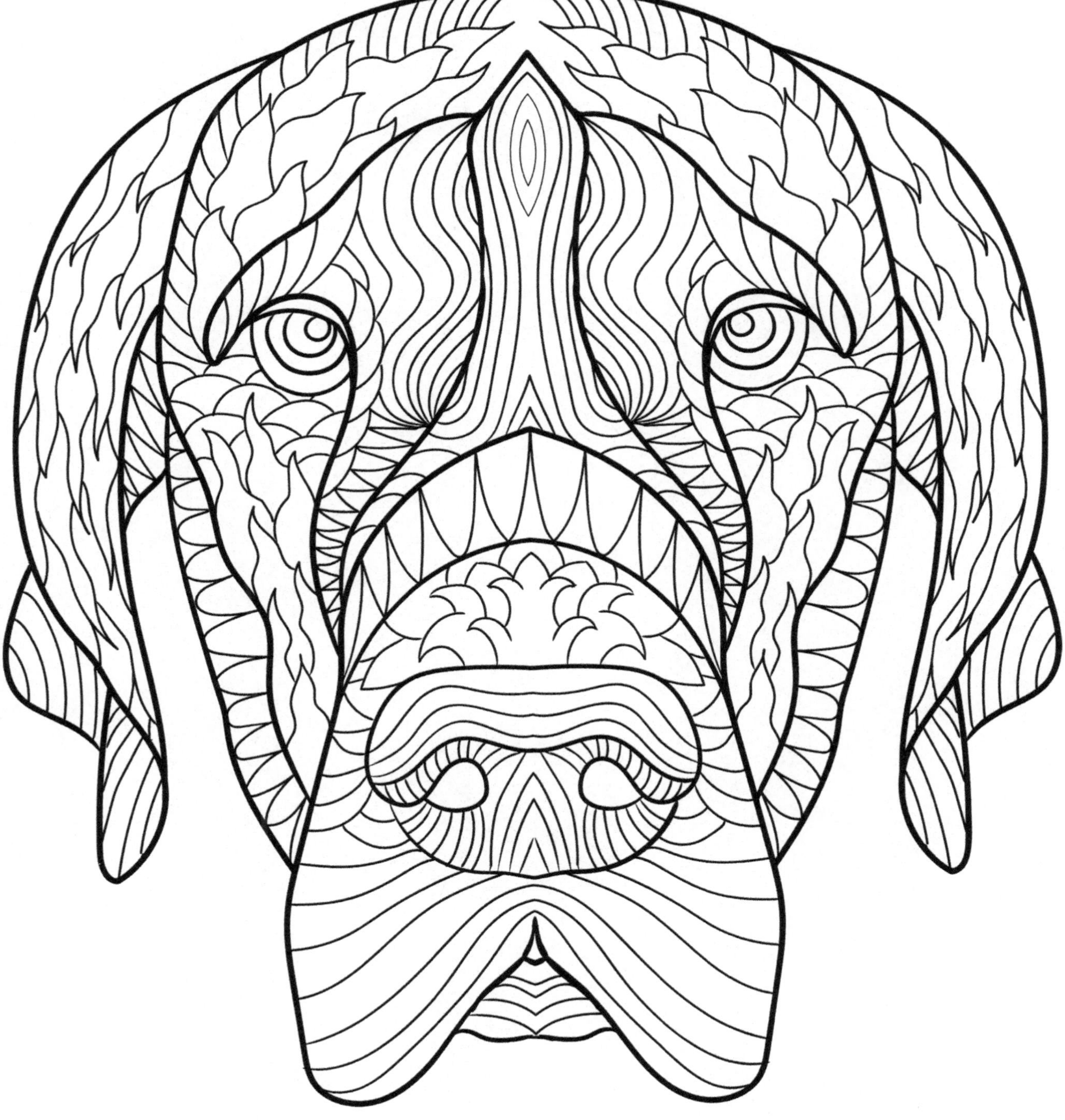

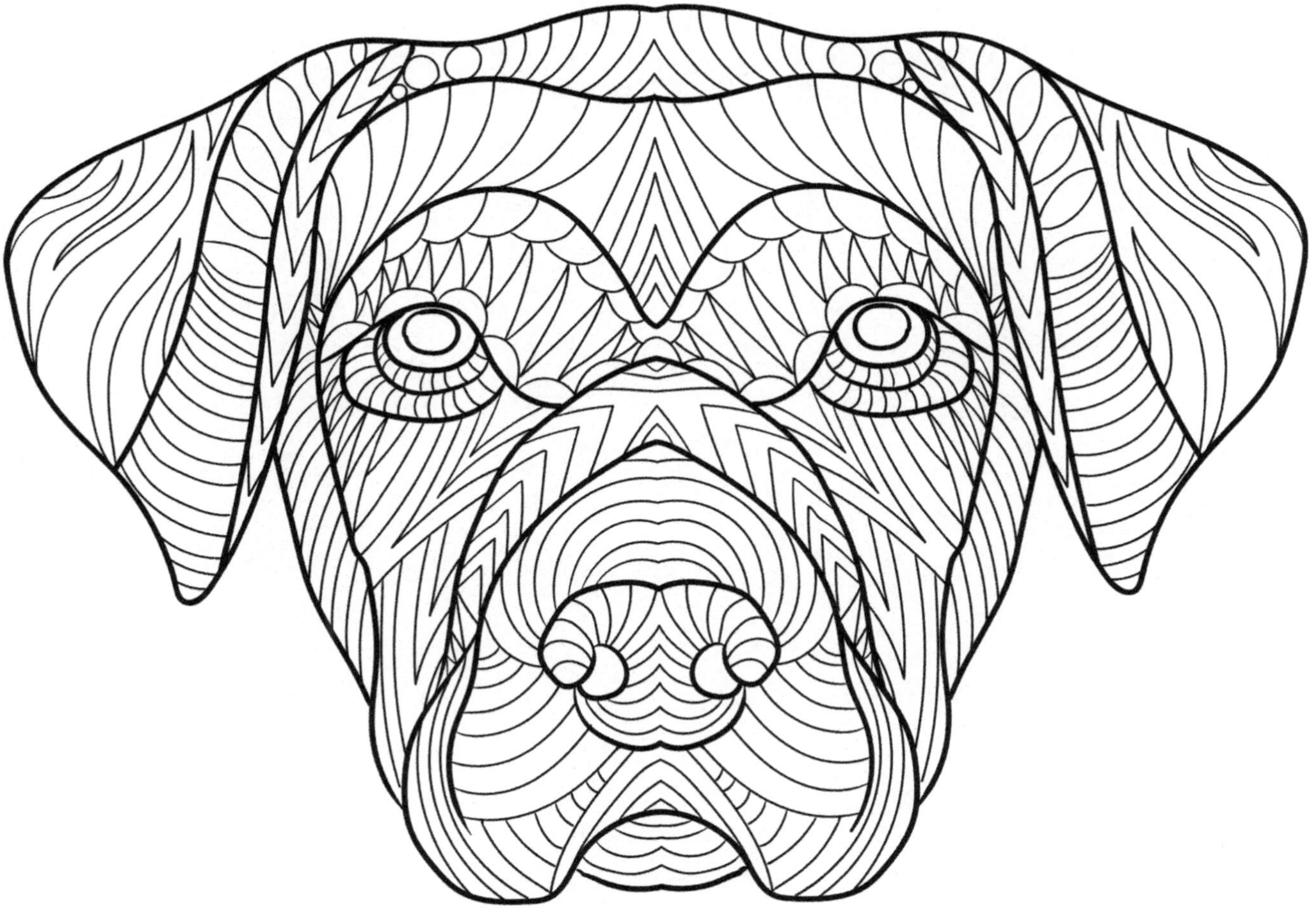

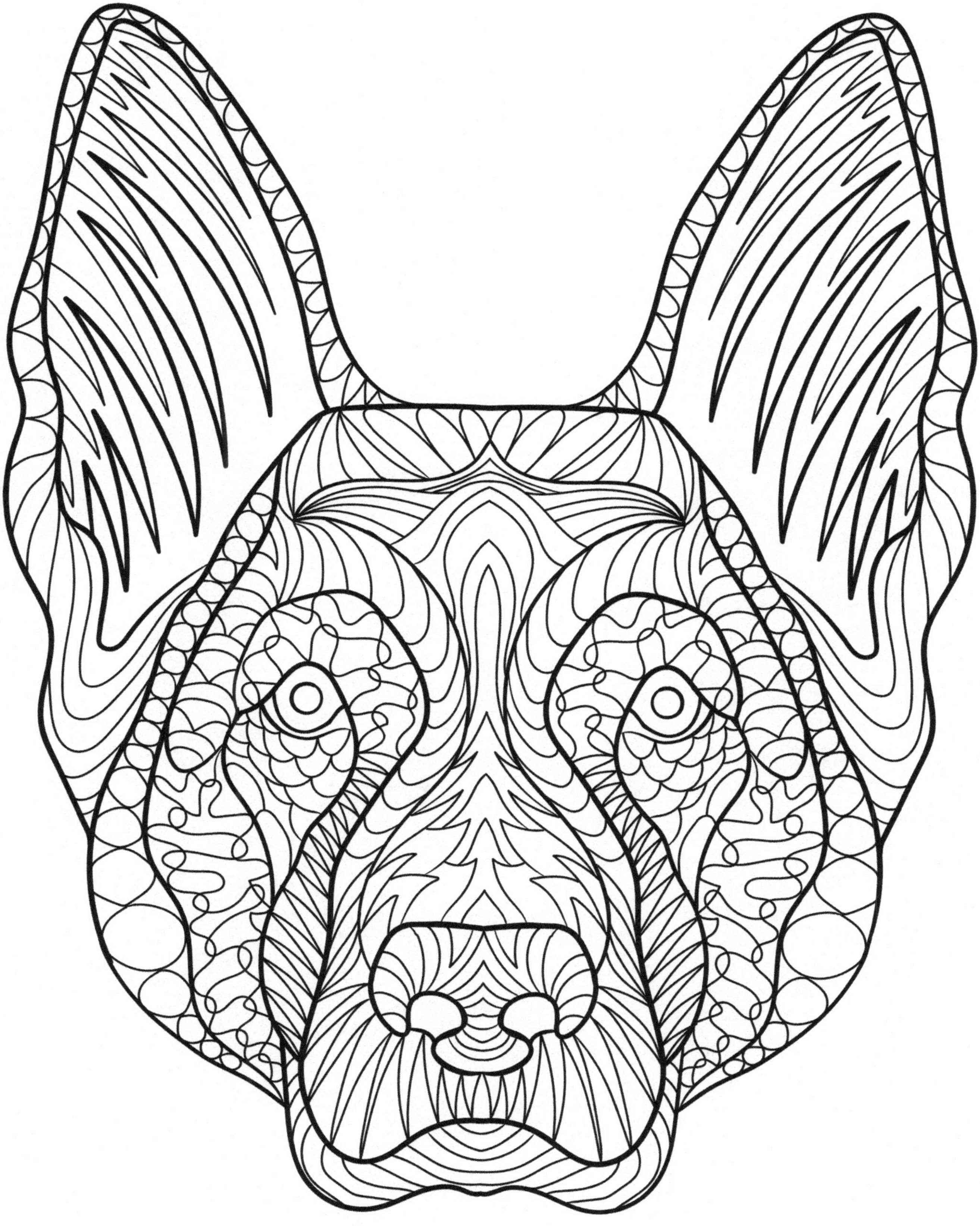

37094672R00027

Made in the USA
Middletown, DE
22 February 2019